MINI HABIT FOR TEENS

Building Small Habits, Big Futures

GBOGO.S.ADEGBOYE

INTRODUCTION

In today's fast-paced teenage world, where every day brings new challenges and opportunities, the pursuit of personal growth and fulfilment can often feel like an uphill battle. From the pressures of academic success to the complexities of social relationships, navigating adolescence requires resilience, determination, and a willingness to embrace change. In the chaos of teenage life, there is a powerful but often overlooked tool that could revolutionize the way young people approach personal development: mini-habits. These small, seemingly insignificant actions can produce significant results over time, paving the way for lasting, transformative success.

In this book, aptly titled "Mini Habits for Teens: Building Small Habits, Big Future," we take a journey into the heart of mini habits and explore their profound impact on the lives of today's teenagers. Drawing upon insights from psychology, neuroscience, and personal development, we uncover the science behind habit formation and its profound impact on teenage development.

Through real-life stories, practical strategies, and actionable advice, we will delve into the art and science of cultivating mini habits that align with teenage goals, values, and aspirations. From academic success to emotional well-being, from healthy relationships to personal growth, we will explore the myriad ways in which mini habits can empower teens to create positive change in every aspect of their lives.

But this book is more than just a guide to habit formation; it is a roadmap to unlocking the full potential that lies within each and every teenager. It is a call to action for young people to take ownership of their habits, their choices, and their futures. It's an invitation to embark on a journey of self-discovery and personal growth, one small habit at a time. Whether you are a teenager who wants to reach their full potential, a parent or educator who wants to empower young people in their lives, or simply someone who believes in the power of small actions to make big changes, this book will help you to achieve them. Together we will embark on a transformative journey into the world of mini-habits and discover the extraordinary opportunities that await us on the way to a better future.

Chapter One

WHAT IS HABIT

In the bustling landscape of teenage life, where every moment seems to be consumed by a whirlwind of activities, responsibilities, and social pressures, the idea of cultivating habits might appear daunting or even inconsequential to many. Yet, nestled within the chaos lies a powerful concept that has the potential to transform the very fabric of our existence: mini habits.

Habits form the cornerstone of our daily lives, shaping our actions, routines, and ultimately, our outcomes. While many of us aspire to adopt new habits or break free from old ones, the task often seems daunting, leading to procrastination or outright abandonment. Enter the concept of "mini habits," a revolutionary approach to habit formation pioneered by author Stephen Guise. Mini habits offer a unique perspective, advocating for the initiation of incredibly small actions to catalyze long-term behavioral change.

A mini habit is a behavior so simple and undemanding that it almost seems insignificant. Rather than setting ambitious goals or overwhelming ourselves with tasks, mini habits encourage individuals to commit to actions that require minimal effort and time. For instance, instead of vowing to write an entire chapter each day, one might commit to writing just one sentence. The beauty of mini habits lies in their ability to bypass the brain's resistance to change by circumventing the usual barriers of motivation and willpower. By lowering the activation energy required to start a task, mini habits make habit formation accessible to anyone, regardless of their circumstances or current level of motivation.

What sets mini habits apart from traditional approaches to habit formation is their emphasis on consistency and incremental progress. While the individual actions may seem trivial, their cumulative effect over time is profound. By consistently engaging in mini habits, individuals gradually build momentum and establish a pattern of success, reinforcing positive behaviors and rewiring neural pathways. The small size of mini habits makes them highly adaptable to busy schedules and fluctuating circumstances, ensuring that progress can be maintained even during challenging times. Ultimately, the transformative power of mini habits lies not in their size, but in their ability to instigate sustainable change through the relentless pursuit of small, manageable actions. mini habits represent a paradigm shift in the realm of habit formation, offering a refreshingly simple yet remarkably effective approach to personal growth. By embracing the philosophy of "smaller is better," individuals can overcome the inertia of inaction and embark on a journey of continuous improvement. Through the consistent practice of tiny actions, anyone can harness the power of mini habits to unlock their full potential and cultivate a life filled with purpose, productivity, and fulfillment.

Imagine, if you will, the profound impact that small, seemingly insignificant actions can have on the trajectory of our lives. Picture a teenager, perhaps struggling with academic challenges, self-doubt, or the overwhelming demands of social expectations. In the midst of this tumult, the notion of implementing mini habits emerges as a beacon of hope, offering a simple yet revolutionary approach to personal growth and self-improvement. But what exactly are mini habits, and why should they matter to today's teenagers? At their core, mini habits are tiny, bite-sized behaviours that require minimal effort and commitment, yet yield remarkable results over time. Unlike traditional approaches to habit formation, which often emphasize radical overhauls or lofty aspirations, mini habits operate on the principle of gradual, sustainable change.

Consider, for instance, the teenager who dreams of excelling academically but finds themselves overwhelmed by the prospect of studying for hours on end. Instead of succumbing to feelings of overwhelm or procrastination, they might embrace the concept of mini habits by committing to just five minutes of focused study each day. In doing so, they not only lower the barrier to entry but also cultivate a sense of consistency and momentum that propels them forward on their academic journey. Indeed, the beauty of mini habits lies in their simplicity and accessibility. Whether it's practicing a musical instrument for a few minutes each day, incorporating daily exercise into one's routine, or dedicating a few moments to mindfulness and reflection, the possibilities are endless. By dividing highly ambitious objectives into smaller, more achievable actions, teenagers can bypass the mental barriers and self-limiting beliefs that often hinder progress.

But perhaps the most compelling aspect of mini habits is their potential to ignite a ripple effect of positive change across every aspect of teenage life. As small victories accumulate and confidence grows, teenagers may find themselves emboldened to tackle increasingly ambitious goals, whether in academics, extracurricular pursuits, or personal relationships.

Moreover, the impact of mini habits extends far beyond the realm of individual achievement, permeating the very fabric of teenage culture and society at large. Imagine a generation of empowered, self-aware teens who approach life with intentionality and purpose, who understand that true transformation begins not with grand gestures or momentous breakthroughs, but with the consistent, relentless pursuit of small, meaningful actions.

In the pages that follow, we will embark on a journey into the heart of mini habits, exploring their potential to revolutionize the way teenagers approach personal development, academic success, and emotional well-being. Through real-life examples, practical strategies, and insightful reflections, we will uncover the untapped power that lies within each of us to effect positive change, one small habit at a time. So, dear reader, I invite you to join me on this transformative quest as we discover the extraordinary possibilities that await us on the path of mini habits.

Chapter Two

UNDERSTANDING ADOLESENT DEVELOPMENT

Adolescence is a period of profound emotional and physical growth. Teenagers making the move from childhood to adulthood, they face countless challenges and opportunities that shape their identities, values, and desires. In this chapter, we examine the unique features of adolescent development and their profound effects on the formation of habits and behaviours.

Adolescence is a period of profound change characterized by a complex interplay of social, psychological, and biological factors. Socially, adolescents navigate peer relationships, societal expectations, and emerging identities. Psychologically, they grapple with issues such as self-esteem, autonomy, and identity formation. Meanwhile, biologically, the adolescent brain undergoes significant remodeling, with neural connections being pruned and refined while new ones are formed. These elements interact dynamically, shaping the experiences and behaviors of adolescents during this crucial developmental stage.

One of the most striking aspects of adolescent development is the remodeling of the brain. During this time, the brain undergoes extensive changes, particularly in regions responsible for functions such as impulse control, mood regulation, and decision-making. The prefrontal cortex, in particular, undergoes significant development during adolescence. This region of the brain is critical for executive functions, including planning, judgment, and self-regulation. As these neural circuits mature, adolescents gain the ability to regulate their emotions, control impulses, and make more informed decisions.

The neurological remodeling that occurs during adolescence has profound implications for emotional regulation and behavior. Adolescents often experience heightened emotional intensity, characterized by mood swings, impulsivity, and sensitivity to social cues. This increased emotional volatility can contribute to risky behaviors such as substance use, reckless driving, and unprotected sex. At the same time, the plasticity of the adolescent brain creates opportunities for habit formation and behavior change. Positive behaviors practiced during this period can become ingrained as habits, shaping long-term patterns of behavior and contributing to overall well-being.

While adolescence is often associated with risk-taking and experimentation, it is also a critical period for habit formation and behavior change. The brain's heightened plasticity during this time makes it particularly receptive to new experiences and learning. Positive behaviors practiced consistently during adolescence, such as regular exercise, healthy eating, and academic diligence, have the potential to become entrenched as lifelong habits. Similarly, interventions aimed at promoting positive behaviors during adolescence, such as education on risk reduction or skill-building programs, can have lasting effects on behavior and well-being.

In summary, adolescence is a period of remarkable growth and change, marked by the interplay of social, psychological, and biological factors. The remodeling of the adolescent brain creates both challenges and opportunities, contributing to heightened emotional intensity, increased risk-taking, and the potential for habit formation and behavior change. Understanding these dynamics is crucial for supporting adolescents as they navigate this transformative stage of development and for promoting positive outcomes in the long term.In fact, teenagers' brains are uniquely equipped to learn and adapt, making adolescence an ideal time to develop positive habits that can last a lifetime. However, this developmental plasticity makes adolescents particularly vulnerable to external influences, including peer pressure, social norms, and media messages. Therefore, it is important to understand the complexities of adolescent development in order to develop effective strategies for habit formation and personal development.

One of the greatest challenges of adolescence is the search for identity and autonomy. As teenagers attempt to define themselves and establish their place in the world, they may experiment with different behaviours, values, and social roles. This pursuit of self-discovery can either facilitate or hinder habit formation, depending on the extent to which adolescents are able to align their habits with their authentic selves and their long-term goals.

Adolescence is also marked by increased susceptibility to peer pressure and social cues. Adolescents frequently place a high value on acceptance and belonging from their peers, which encourages them to copy the good and bad behaviors and routines of their peers. Therefore, in order to create a supportive environment that encourages healthy behaviors and positive choices, it is essential to grasp the dynamics of peer influence. Adolescents' ideas, attitudes, and behaviors are shaped by larger cultural and environmental circumstances in addition to biological and social variables. The external factors influencing teenage growth are numerous and varied, ranging from media portrayals and cultural standards to family relationships and socioeconomic condition. In order to create interventions and strategies that are sensitive to the experiences of young people, it is imperative to acknowledge the significance of these contextual elements.

Growing up is a dynamic process that is always changing, filled with obstacles as well as chances for development. We can create a customized strategy for forming habits that help teenagers thrive in all facets of their lives by comprehending the intricacies of adolescent development and taking use of the special qualities of their brains. The upcoming chapters will delve into useful tactics and concepts for utilizing youth development to foster short-term routines that result in long-term development and transformation.

Chapter Three

SETTING THE STAGE OF SUCCESS

In the quest for personal growth and achievement, clarity of purpose and direction is paramount. As teenagers navigate the complexities of adolescence, they are faced with a myriad of choices and opportunities, each with the potential to shape their futures in profound ways. In this chapter, we delve into the importance of setting clear goals and aspirations as the foundation for successful habit formation and personal development.

"What do I want to achieve?" is the fundamental question at the center of goal setting. This topic can cover a wide range of goals for teenagers, from relationships and mental health to job aspirations and academic achievement. Nevertheless, many youngsters may find themselves lost in the din of competing voices, unclear of their genuine interests and objectives.

This is the point at which self-awareness and introspection become useful. Teenagers can acquire clarity and insight into what really important to them by reflecting on their beliefs, hobbies, and long-term goals. Setting objectives that are meaningful, genuine, and in line with one's inner principles is made possible by the process of self-discovery, which can be accomplished through writing, meditation, or in-depth discussions with trustworthy mentors.

Setting goals, however, involves more than just seeing a far-off place; it also involves deciding on a path of action that will help one go from where they are to where they want to be. Here's where the idea of "keystone habits" really pays off. Little, fundamental behaviors known as "keystone habits" have a significant impact on other facets of life. Teens can initiate good change that has a cascading effect on their life by recognizing and prioritizing keystone habits.

Developing a growth mindset is crucial for surviving the turbulent adolescent years. In a world where obstacles are unavoidable and success expectations sometimes seem overpowering, having faith in one's capacity to develop and adapt serves as a strong anchor during difficult times.

Teenagers are continuously presented with new difficulties and chances for personal development during their adolescent years, which are a time of great transformation and discovery. Teenagers face innumerable challenges that put their will and determination to the test, whether it's passing a challenging exam, learning a new skill, or navigating the complexities of peer relationships. A growth mindset offers teens hope during these trying times by reassuring them that their skills are flexible rather than fixed and that, with enough work and dedication, they can overcome any obstacle and realize their objectives.

Accepting obstacles is the foundation of a growth mentality. Teenagers that have a growth mindset view obstacles as chances for personal development and education rather than running away from problems or being afraid of failing. They realize that obstacles are only normal stops along the way to becoming an expert, not a reflection of their inherent skills. Rather of perceiving failure as an indication of insufficiency, they regard it as an invaluable source of feedback and comprehension that directs them towards enhanced comprehension and advancement.

Furthermore, growth-minded youth recognize the value of tenacity in the face of difficulty. They understand that growth frequently calls for grit, patience, and resilience—that success is not always instantaneous or linear. When faced with challenges or failures, they don't give up in defeat but instead intensify their efforts, utilizing every setback as motivation to go on their path to success and personal development.

Another indicator of a growth mentality is the celebration of accomplishments, no matter how modest. Teens with a growth mindset take pride in their accomplishments and acknowledge the hard work and effort that went into getting there, as opposed to downplaying or attributing them to chance or circumstance alone. They enhance their confidence to take on even bigger challenges in the future and strengthen their trust in their potential to succeed by acknowledging and applauding their accomplishments along the road.

Basically, encouraging resilience and optimism in teenagers is what it means to cultivate a growth mindset. This helps them on their path to success and personal development. It is about giving children the idea that anything is possible and that they can accomplish their goals and conquer any challenge if they work hard, are persistent, and have the correct attitude. Teenagers may develop a mindset that will enable them to succeed in all facets of their lives, both now and in the future, by embracing difficulties, learning from mistakes, and appreciating accomplishments along the way.

Teens who want to do well in school, for instance, might view regular study habits as a foundational behavior that helps them succeed in other areas like time management, stress management, and self-discipline. Adolescents who aim to enhance their physical well-being might consider regular exercise as a fundamental habit that promotes mental toughness, self-assurance, and physical health. Teenagers must develop a growth mindset, which is the conviction that their skills and intelligence can be enhanced via hard work and persistence, in addition to goal-setting and keystone habits. Teenagers can cultivate a sense of resilience and optimism that drives their path toward personal growth and achievement by accepting obstacles, learning from setbacks, and appreciating victories along the road.

Setting objectives and developing keystone behaviors is also a communal, iterative process that calls for accountability and support from others rather than being an isolated undertaking. Teenagers flourish when they have a network of allies that encourage and assist them along the way, hold them accountable, and cheer them on, whether through peer groups, mentors, or sympathetic family members.

In the ensuing chapters, we will delve into useful tactics and applicable perspectives for establishing and accomplishing objectives, developing foundational routines, and promoting a development mindset that enables adolescents to realize their complete potential. By creating the foundation for success now, we open the door to a future full of meaning, fulfillment, and boundless opportunities.

Chapter Four

DESIGNING YOUR MINI HABIT

In the intricate tapestry of personal development, habits serve as the threads that weave together the fabric of our lives. From the moment we wake until we retire to bed, our actions and behaviors are governed by an intricate web of habits, both conscious and unconscious. For teenagers embarking on the journey of self-discovery and growth, the cultivation of positive habits is not merely a choice but a necessity—a pathway to unlocking their full potential and shaping the trajectory of their futures.

However, what are habits really, and how can we develop them? Fundamentally, habits are the reflexive, automatic actions that mold our everyday schedules and impact our long-term results. Habits are engrained patterns of behavior that direct our behaviors with little conscious thought, such as brushing our teeth in the morning, checking our phones before bed, or practicing an instrument.

A novel approach to habit formation is provided by the idea of "mini habits," which places an emphasis on sustainability, consistency, and simplicity rather than dramatic changes or showy gestures. By focusing on small, manageable behaviors that may be easily adopted into everyday routines, mini habits operate on the premise of "small steps, big impact," in contrast to traditional techniques that frequently emphasize drive and willpower.

So how can we create our own little routines? Our objectives, beliefs, and aspirations must be thoroughly understood before we can begin the process. Establishing a clear understanding of our goals and the reasons behind them helps us make decisions about behaviors that support our future vision. Making decisions based on our deepest wishes and objectives is crucial, whether the goal is to improve our academic achievement, improve our physical health, or nurture our emotional well-being.

Certainly, let's delve deeper into the concept of cultivating a growth mindset and its significance for teenagers navigating the challenges of adolescence.

Embracing Challenges:

 Adolescence is a time of significant growth and development, both academically and personally. Teenagers face a myriad of challenges, from academic pressures to social dynamics and identity formation. A growth mindset teaches teenagers to view these challenges not as insurmountable obstacles, but as opportunities for learning and growth. Instead of feeling defeated by setbacks or failures, they see them as valuable experiences that can lead to greater understanding and resilience. For example, if a teenager struggles with a difficult math problem, a growth mindset encourages them to approach it with curiosity and perseverance, knowing that each attempt brings them closer to mastery.

Learning from Failures:

Failure is an inevitable part of life, but it's how we respond to failure that shapes our growth and development. Teenagers with a growth mindset understand that failure is not a reflection of their intelligence or abilities, but a natural part of the learning process. Rather than dwelling on their mistakes or giving up in frustration, they use failure as an opportunity for reflection and growth. For instance, if a teenager receives a low grade on a test, instead of feeling discouraged, they might analyze their mistakes, seek help from a teacher or tutor, and develop a plan to improve their performance in the future.

Celebrating Successes:

In a culture that often emphasizes perfectionism and achievement, it's easy for teenagers to downplay their successes or feel like they're never doing enough. However, a growth mindset encourages teenagers to celebrate their accomplishments, no matter how small. By acknowledging their progress and recognizing their efforts, teenagers build confidence in their abilities and develop a sense of self-efficacy. For example, if a teenager completes a challenging assignment or learns a new skill, celebrating that achievement reinforces their belief in their capacity to succeed and motivates them to continue striving for excellence.

Cultivating a growth mindset empowers teenagers to embrace challenges, learn from failures, and celebrate successes along their journey of personal growth and achievement. By fostering resilience, optimism, and a belief in their own potential, a growth mindset equips teenagers with the mindset and tools they need to thrive in the face of adversity and create a future filled with purpose and possibility.We could practice yoga stretches, go for a little stroll, or perform a few push-ups. We lower entrance barriers and build momentum that advances us on our fitness path by making the habit so small that it seems nearly effortless.
Effective mini habits are not just little and manageable, but also targeted and practical. Instead of establishing ambiguous objectives such as "gain

physical fitness" or "increase productivity," we must be specific and detailed in outlining the behaviors we want to engage in. Whether our habits are as simple as "write one paragraph in a journal each morning" or as complex as "read one chapter of a book before bed," the important thing is to make them obvious, doable, and accessible. Effective mini habits are also easily incorporated into our daily lives because they are rooted in our current routines and surroundings. The idea is to establish cues and triggers that cause us to act without needing to rely solely on motivation or willpower, whether that means attaching our new habit to a certain time of day, place, or previous behavior.

We will go deeper into the science and art of creating micro habits that work in the ensuing chapters, including doable tactics for choosing, putting into practice, and maintaining habits that bring about long-term fulfillment and change. Teens may unleash the potential of tiny actions to bring about significant changes in all facets of their lives by learning the concepts of habit design.

Chapter Five

IMPLEMENTING MINI HABITS IN TEEN LIFE

In the dynamic landscape of teenage life, where every day brings new challenges and opportunities, the implementation of mini habits is not merely an abstract concept but a practical and tangible endeavor. As teenagers navigate the complexities of academics, extracurricular activities, social relationships, and personal growth, the integration of small, manageable actions into their daily routines becomes essential for fostering positive change and achieving long-term success.

What is the process by which teenagers adopt small routines in their hectic and frequently erratic lives? The secret is to develop a purposeful, consistent, and adaptive attitude that is open to trying new things and accepting change in the face of difficulties and disappointments.

Making a detailed action plan is one of the first steps in putting small habits into practice. This entails figuring out whether particular habits are in line with one's objectives and moral principles as well as scheduling the how, when, and where these habits will be carried out. The idea is to provide a systematic framework that facilitates continuous behavior change, whether that framework takes the form of allocating a certain time slot for study sessions, designating a room for artistic endeavors, or using daily routines as cues for new habits. Moreover, some level of self-awareness and self-discipline are necessary for the successful application of habits. Adolescents need to learn to identify the triggers and temptations that could impede their growth, in addition to their own thought and behavior patterns. Teenagers who practice mindfulness and self-reflection will be better able to recognize their tendencies and make deliberate decisions that will help them achieve their personal objectives.

Accountability is as important to habit implementation as self-awareness. In difficult circumstances, having outside sources of accountability can offer perspective, encouragement, and motivation. This can be achieved by asking friends, family, or mentors for help. Teens can use the power of community to remain on track and accomplish their objectives by doing anything from sharing progress updates with a trusted confidante to taking part in group challenges or accountability partnerships. Moreover, the capacity to be flexible and adaptable is crucial for teens to successfully adopt little behaviors. Teens must learn to modify their habits and routines in response to changing priorities, schedules, and circumstances because adolescence is a time of perpetual change and transition. Maintaining momentum and keeping on course requires the capacity to pivot and readjust while dealing with unforeseen occurrences, changing school schedules, or overcoming obstacles. Perhaps most crucially, developing small habits calls for a resilient and self-compassionate mindset. Adolescents need to learn to be kind to themselves, understanding that life is not always a straight line and that obstacles are a normal part of the path to development and success. Teens can learn from their mistakes, overcome setbacks, and move forward with redoubled resolve if they are able to develop resilience and tenacity.

The chapters that follow will cover useful tactics and applicable knowledge for putting small habits into practice in a variety of adolescent contexts, such as academics, extracurricular activities, interpersonal relationships, and mental health. Teens may unleash the power of tiny actions to bring about significant change and build a future full of meaning, fulfillment, and endless opportunities by learning the art of habit implementation.

Chapter Six

OVERCOMING CHALLENGES AND STAYING MOTIVATED

In the pursuit of personal growth and achievement, challenges and obstacles are inevitable companions on the journey. For teenagers embarking on the path of habit formation and self-improvement, the road ahead is fraught with potential pitfalls, from procrastination and self-doubt to external pressures and unexpected setbacks. In this chapter, we explore strategies for overcoming challenges and staying motivated in the face of adversity.

Teenagers frequently encounter difficulties forming mini-habits due to the constant tug of conflicting demands and distractions. Finding the time and energy to concentrate on new habits can feel like an uphill fight when social media, extracurricular activities, and academic obligations compete for their attention. In order to overcome this obstacle, teenagers need to develop time management skills and prioritize their objectives. They also need to carve out certain windows of time among the chaos and bustle of adolescence to create new habits. Furthermore, even the best-intentioned attempts to create new habits can be derailed by the urge to put things off or give in to the need for instant satisfaction. Teens need to learn how to identify and fight the impulse to put off tasks, such as choosing to study instead of going for a morning run or hitting the snooze button instead of studying. They also need to learn to replace ineffective behaviors with more productive ones.

Teens may experience external expectations and pressures in addition to internal struggles that thwart their attempts to form small habits. Teens need to have the resilience and self-assurance to deal with outside pressures, such as parental expectations that conflict with their own beliefs and goals or peer pressure to adopt unhealthy habits. Teens can navigate the challenges of life and find personal fulfillment by remaining loyal to themselves and their objectives.

Failures and setbacks are an unavoidable aspect of the process of forming habits. Setbacks can be disheartening and demoralizing, whether they involve missing a practice day, not reaching a goal, or running into unforeseen difficulties. Teens must learn to reframe failures as opportunities for learning and growth, rather than seeing them as insurmountable obstacles. Teenagers who embrace a growth mindset and see losses as insightful learning opportunities can overcome obstacles with redoubled resolve and tenacity.

For teens starting the process of forming new

habits, staying motivated over the long run can also be difficult. Teens may experience a decline in initial zeal and excitement over time, which can leave them feeling demotivated and inspired to continue their habits. Teens need to develop intrinsic motivation—the inner zeal and drive that keeps them going even in the absence of outside rewards—to combat this. Cultivating intrinsic motivation is crucial for long-term habit retention. This can be achieved by emphasizing the intrinsic advantages of habit formation, such as personal development and self-improvement, or by finding joy and satisfaction in the process of habit creation itself.

In the ensuing chapters, we will delve into useful tactics and applicable perspectives for surmounting obstacles and maintaining motivation while pursuing microhabits. Teenagers may overcome challenges, persevere, and eventually accomplish their goals by developing the skills of resilience, self-discipline, and intrinsic motivation. This will pave the way for a future full of meaning, fulfillment, and endless opportunities.

Chapter Seven

NUTURING WELL-BEING THROUGH MINI HABIT

In the fast-paced and often tumultuous landscape of teenage life, prioritizing well-being can sometimes feel like an elusive goal. From the pressures of academic success to the complexities of social relationships, teenagers face a myriad of challenges that can take a toll on their mental, emotional, and physical health. In this chapter, we explore the transformative potential of mini habits in nurturing well-being and fostering resilience in the face of adversity.

Well-being is a comprehensive approach to health that includes emotional fortitude, social connectedness, physical fitness, and a sense of fulfillment and purpose in life. Developing habits that support wellbeing is crucial for teenagers navigating the highs and lows of adolescence in order to deal with the difficulties of puberty with grace and resilience.

Mini habits have the potential to greatly enhance well-being by cultivating mindfulness and self-awareness, among other things. Teens can develop a better awareness of their thoughts, feelings, and emotions by incorporating mindfulness practices into their daily routine. Some examples of these practices include meditating for a short while in the morning, practicing gratitude before bed, and taking frequent breaks during the day to check in with themselves.

Mini habits can also be quite helpful in reducing stress and fostering emotional stability. Little, consistent actions can have a big impact on one's capacity to handle the inevitable challenges and stressors of teenage life, whether it's journaling to process thoughts and emotions, practicing relaxation techniques to unwind after a long day, or deep breathing exercises to calm the nervous system.

Mini habits can be quite important for fostering physical health and energy in addition to fostering mental well-being. Making healthier dietary choices, getting regular exercise, or stressing the need of getting enough sleep and staying hydrated are just a few examples of how simple, sustained behavioral adjustments may have a big impact on one's general health and well-being.

Mini habits can also help teenagers feel more connected to others and more a part of the community, which is important for their wellbeing as they navigate the complicated dynamics of peer interactions and society. Simple actions of compassion and connection, such as contacting a friend, joining a club or sports team, or volunteering in the community, can build social ties and a support system that increases resilience and promotes a sense of belonging.

We shall examine useful tactics and applicable knowledge for promoting wellbeing through tiny routines in the ensuing chapters. Teens can develop habits that promote their overall well-being and set the stage for a future full of purpose, fulfillment, and resilience in the face of adversity by placing a high priority on mindfulness, emotional resilience, physical health, and social connectedness.

Chapter Eight

MINI HABITS FOR ACADEMIC SUCCESS

In the realm of teenage life, few domains hold as much significance and impact as academic achievement. From college admissions and career opportunities to personal fulfillment and intellectual growth, academic success lays the groundwork for a future filled with possibilities. In this chapter, we explore the transformative potential of mini habits in fostering academic excellence and unlocking the full potential of teenage learners.

Academic success is fundamentally about developing an attitude of curiosity, critical thinking, and lifelong learning rather than just getting good grades or mastering subject matter. Teenagers who adopt mini habits have a strong foundation for acquiring these traits, which enables them to take charge of their education and pursue knowledge with a strong sense of purpose and passion.

Encouraging consistent and productive study habits is one of the best ways that small habits may assist academic performance. Little, regular actions can have a big impact on learning outcomes. Some examples of these actions include reviewing class notes, practicing problem-solving strategies, and breaking down larger assignments into smaller, more manageable ones. All of these activities should be done for a few minutes each day. Developing tiny habits can be very helpful in fostering the development of critical academic abilities like self-control, organization, and time management. Teens can cultivate the mentality and work ethic required for academic achievement by implementing practices like making study schedules, utilizing productivity tools like the Pomodoro technique, and setting clear goals for their studies.

Mini habits can help promote a growth mindset, which is the conviction that aptitude and intelligence can be enhanced with effort and persistence, in addition to academic capabilities. Teenagers can develop a mindset that will enable them to overcome barriers and succeed academically by rephrasing setbacks as chances for growth, asking for and accepting constructive criticism, and appreciating the learning process itself.

Mini habits can also improve general academic well-being by fostering emotional resilience and stress management. Small, regular acts can help teens deal with the inevitable ups and downs of academic life with grace and resilience. Some examples of these actions include practicing relaxation techniques before tests, asking peers and mentors for support, and participating in self-care activities to recharge and revitalize.

The ensuing chapters will delve into useful tactics and applicable perspectives for integrating small routines into diverse facets of school life, ranging from time management and study habits to exam planning and continuous education. Teenagers can realize their full academic potential and set the stage for a future full of intellectual curiosity, academic brilliance, and lifetime success by developing the skill of habit formation and adopting a growth mindset.

Chapter Nine

BUILDING HEALTHY RELATIONSHIP AND SOCIAL

In the intricate tapestry of teenage life, relationships and social dynamics play a central role in shaping identity, self-esteem, and emotional well-being. From friendships and family bonds to romantic relationships and peer interactions, the connections we forge with others profoundly impact our sense of belonging and fulfillment. In this chapter, we explore the transformative potential of mini habits in building healthy relationships and fostering social skills that empower teenagers to navigate the complexities of human connection with grace and authenticity.

At the heart of healthy relationships lies a foundation of communication, empathy, and mutual respect. Mini habits offer a powerful framework for cultivating these essential qualities, empowering teenagers to develop the interpersonal skills necessary for building strong, meaningful connections with others.

One of the most effective ways in which mini habits can support healthy relationships is by promoting active listening and effective communication. Whether it's setting aside dedicated time each day to have meaningful conversations with family members, practicing reflective listening techniques to better understand the perspectives of others, or expressing appreciation and gratitude through small, thoughtful gestures, teenagers can cultivate habits that foster open, honest, and empathetic communication.

Mini habits can play a crucial role in nurturing empathy and compassion—the ability to understand and empathize with the thoughts, feelings, and experiences of others. Whether it's performing acts of kindness and generosity, volunteering in the community, or engaging in perspective-taking exercises to broaden one's understanding of different viewpoints, small, consistent actions can help teenagers develop a deeper sense of empathy and connection with others.

Mini habits can improve conflict resolution abilities and foster constructive conflict resolution in addition to encouraging empathy and healthy communication. Teenagers can handle conflicts with grace and maturity, bolstering relationships and promoting mutual understanding and respect, by adopting practices like taking deep breaths and practicing mindfulness during heated discussions, using "I" statements to express feelings and needs, and looking for win-win solutions.

Mini habits can also help people feel connected to and included in their peer groups and social networks. Teens can develop and sustain meaningful connections that enrich their lives and give them a sense of community and belonging by taking small, consistent actions, such as checking in and offering support to a friend, striking up a conversation with a new acquaintance, or joining in group activities and events.

We will look at doable tactics and useful insights for implementing mini-habits into many facets of social interaction and relationship-building in the upcoming chapters. Teenagers can develop positive connections and social skills that enable them to confidently, authentically, and resiliently negotiate the difficulties of human connection by developing their communication, empathy, and conflict resolution abilities.

Chapter Ten

EMBRACING LIFE'S CHALLENGES

Life is a journey filled with twists and turns, triumphs and setbacks, joys and sorrows. Along the way, we encounter obstacles and challenges that test our resolve, shake our confidence, and push us to our limits. In this final chapter, we explore the transformative power of mini habits in cultivating resilience—the ability to bounce back from adversity, adapt to change, and thrive in the face of life's challenges.

Resilience is really about accepting life's obstacles as chances for personal development and evolution, rather than just surviving adversity or storms. It is about developing a strong, adaptable, and positive mindset that enables us to go through challenges and come out stronger and more resilient than before. Mini habits provide a strong framework for developing these vital traits, giving us the ability to face life's obstacles with bravery, grace, and resilience.

Mini routines that encourage mental health and self-care are among the best methods to build resilience. Our foundation of emotional resilience can withstand life's ups and downs by embracing habits like mindfulness and meditation, physical activity, and the pursuit of hobbies and interests that offer us joy and fulfillment. Small, frequent acts can help us stay balanced and maintain perspective even in the face of hardship. Examples of these activities include taking regular breaks to rest and recharge, asking for help from loved ones, and engaging in self-compassion and self-care. Mini habits can also be quite helpful in reinterpreting setbacks as chances for development and education. Through the integration of behaviors like actively pursuing novel experiences, establishing audacious objectives, and accepting failure as an inherent aspect of the educational journey, we can foster a growth mindset that enables us to endure adversity. A resilient and upbeat mindset can be developed by little, regular acts like thinking back on our experiences, asking for and accepting constructive criticism, and acknowledging our successes. These activities can aid us on our path to personal development and fulfillment.

Mini habits not only encourage self-care and a growth mentality, but they can also improve our capacity for change and uncertainty adaptation. We may negotiate life's transitions with confidence and resilience if we adopt habits like accepting new difficulties, developing flexibility and adaptability, and looking for chances for learning and progress.

By taking little, regular steps—like venturing outside of our comfort zones, picking up new skills, and seeking out new experiences—we may learn to accept change as a normal part of life and take advantage of the chances it offers for personal development.

Mini habits can also strengthen our resilience in difficult circumstances by fostering a sense of support and community. Small, regular acts can help us create and maintain a support system that helps us overcome obstacles in life and celebrates our victories. These actions can be reaching out to friends and family for support, taking part in group activities and events, or giving back to our communities through acts of kindness and service. In the ensuing chapters, we will delve into useful tactics and applicable perspectives for integrating mini-habits into our everyday routines to foster resilience. We may overcome life's obstacles with grace, bravery, and resilience if we learn the skills of self-care, growth mindset, adaptation, and community support. As a result, we will be stronger and more resilient than before.

Chapter Eleven

INTEGRATING AWARENESS INTO EVERYDAY LIFE

Being totally present and involved in the present moment is a technique known as mindfulness, and it has received a lot of attention for its beneficial effects on adolescent wellbeing. It is a useful tool for overcoming the difficulties of puberty because of its numerous advantages, which include lowering tension and anxiety as well as improving focus and emotional resilience. Teens who practice mindfulness can become more conscious of their thoughts, feelings, and bodily sensations, which will help them handle life's ups and downs more gracefully and easily.

Through our investigation into mindfulness, we unearth doable tactics that enable youngsters to practice mindfulness on a regular basis. Basic breathing techniques are fundamental activities that support youngsters in calming their brains and establishing a sense of groundedness in the midst of the everyday stress. Teenagers can also practice being totally present and attentive to the sensations and experiences of the moment while eating or walking, as these activities are examples of ordinary activities that incorporate mindfulness.

Teenagers can develop a sense of clarity and calmness amidst life's hardships by practicing mindfulness, which teaches them to cultivate greater awareness and present in each moment. Teenagers can handle challenging situations with more composure and resilience by practicing mindfulness, which lowers stress and anxiety levels in them. Additionally, teens who practice mindfulness are better able to concentrate and focus, which allows them to participate more completely in their extracurricular activities, academic pursuits, and interpersonal interactions.

In the end, our investigation into mindfulness highlights its significant influence on adolescent wellbeing and provides a transforming tool for gracefully and easily negotiating the challenges of adolescence. Teenagers can develop a stronger bond with the world and with themselves by introducing mindfulness into their daily routines. This will increase their emotional stability, resilience, and sense of purpose in life.

Chapter Twelve

NAVIGAING THE CHALLENGES OF TECHNOLOGY

Teens face several difficulties in navigating their relationship with technology in the modern digital world. The widespread use of digital devices and online platforms offers never-before-seen chances for entertainment, education, and connection, but it also carries a number of risks that may have an adverse effect on the wellbeing of teenagers. This chapter explores the idea of digital wellness, which is a comprehensive strategy for controlling one's interaction with technology in a way that supports equilibrium and general health.

Establishing reasonable limits on screen time and digital usage is essential to the idea of digital wellbeing. Many kids find themselves spending excessive amounts of time online due to the continual temptation to be connected and plugged in, which can have a detrimental effect on their physical, mental, and emotional well-being. Teenagers can make time for other interests and activities that improve their general well-being, like physical activity, social contacts, and creative hobbies, by setting clear rules for screen time and digital usage.

Digital wellness also includes setting limits, taking digital detoxes, and using tech with awareness. Teenagers who take regular breaks from their digital gadgets are more likely to feel less stressed, anxious, and overwhelmed. Teenagers can also develop a better relationship with technology and keep its negative effects from taking over their lives by practicing mindfulness when using it. This includes being deliberate about when and how they use digital devices, as well as being aware of their online behavior and consumption.

This chapter offers helpful advice and methods for encouraging teens to have a positive relationship with technology and to maintain balance in their life. Through the implementation of mindfulness practices during screen time and the scheduling of regular digital detox days, we enable youngsters to take charge of their digital habits and prioritize their well-being in an increasingly digital environment. Teens can take use of technology's advantages while reducing its possible risks by adopting digital wellness practices, which will help them live more balanced and satisfying lives both online and off.

Chapter Thirteen

BUILDING RESILENCE RELATIONSHIP

Peer interactions are essential to adolescence and have a profound impact on a range of areas of the development and well-being of teenagers. This chapter examines the significant influence that peer interactions have on teenagers, including how they affect their identity formation, behavioral choices, decision-making processes, and sense of self. Teenagers can better grasp the dynamics at work in their relationships and social interactions by realizing the crucial role that peers play in their life.

We explore the difficulties that teenagers encounter in navigating their social environment by delving into the intricacies of peer pressure and social dynamics. Teenagers' behavior and decisions can be greatly influenced by peer pressure in particular, which frequently prompts them to act riskily or comply to social standards. Teenagers can acquire the knowledge and resilience necessary to fend off harmful influences and make decisions that are consistent with their values and objectives by investigating the subtleties of peer pressure and how it affects decision-making.

Teens need to develop strong connections based on communication, authenticity, and respect in order to succeed in their social settings. This chapter provides advice and techniques for building wholesome, encouraging interactions that foster the development and wellbeing of teenagers. Teenagers can develop relationships with peers that are based on mutual respect and trust by encouraging open and honest communication, setting limits, and exercising empathy and understanding. These connections can serve as a source of support and strength during trying times.

Teens will inevitably have to deal with peer conflict, but they may learn positive conflict resolution techniques and build stronger connections in the process. Teenagers can acquire these skills with the correct mentality and approach. Teenagers are better equipped to handle arguments and misunderstandings with maturity and compassion when we teach them conflict resolution techniques like active listening, perspective-taking, and compromise. This promotes stronger bonds and understanding between parties.

In the end, we provide teenagers the tools they need to handle the intricacies of peer relationships with confidence and integrity by giving them the ability to resist harmful influences and build strong, supportive relationships. Teens can develop relationships with peers that support their development, well-being, and sense of identity in the social world by being self-aware, empathic, and communicatively skilled.

Chapter Fourteen

FINDING PURPOSE AND PASSION

Developing a feeling of purpose and passion becomes crucial as youngsters negotiate the challenges of adolescence and start thinking about their futures. We go into great detail in this chapter about how important it is to match one's values, interests, and strengths with their personal and professional goals. Teens can obtain insight into their passions and abilities by starting a self-discovery journey, which paves the way for a happy and prosperous future.

A critical phase in the process of self-discovery and career exploration is investigating educational and employment choices. This chapter offers teens useful advice on how to investigate numerous job options, learn about different businesses and professions, and consider possible school tracks that fit their interests and objectives. Teenagers can increase their alternatives and find possible job pathways that align with their hobbies and objectives by widening their horizons and exploring a variety of opportunities.

Cultivating a sense of purpose and passion requires

knowing one's values, interests, and strengths. We provide them with exercises and advice in this chapter to help them explore their interests, pinpoint their abilities, and define their basic principles. Teenagers can start to envisage a future that is in line with their true self by developing a deeper awareness of who they are and what matters to them. This will help them make decisions and take actions that will lead to greater success and fulfillment.

The process of self-discovery culminates in the translation of interests, strengths, and values into meaningful career pathways and personal pursuits. This chapter looks at doable tactics that teens can use to close the gap between their dreams and reality by establishing specific objectives and moving forward with their plans. Teens may actively create opportunities to explore their interests and talents, setting the path for a purposeful and fulfilling future. This can be done through pursuing internships and volunteer work, enrolling in classes or workshops, or starting side projects and passion projects.

In the end, we provide teenagers the tools they need to succeed in both their personal and professional lives by enabling them to steer toward a future that is in line with their passions, interests, and values.

Teenagers can develop a sense of purpose and passion that directs their journey forward and leads to a future full of meaning, fulfillment, and achievement via self-reflection, discovery, and action.

Chapter Fifteen

CULTIVATING GRATITUDE AND GENEROSITY

One cannot stress the value of developing an attitude of thankfulness and generosity in a culture that frequently places a premium on individual accomplishment and financial success. These attributes are fundamental building blocks that support the development of empathy, compassion, and connection in social and private contexts. This chapter explores the tremendous effects that generosity and thankfulness can have on adolescent mental health and interpersonal relationships while offering doable methods for introducing these virtues into everyday life.

Gratitude is a powerful remedy for negativity and dissatisfaction because it is the act of recognizing and appreciating life's benefits and positive features. Teenagers can develop a stronger feeling of joy, fulfillment, and resilience even in the midst of adversity by adopting an attitude of appreciation. In order to empower teenagers to develop a habit of appreciation that enhances their lives and fosters emotional well-being, we cover a variety of gratitude-related practices in this chapter, including journaling and giving thanks to others.

The act of being generous, or freely giving of oneself to others, is another crucial element in developing compassion, empathy, and connection. Adolescents can develop a sense of fulfillment and purpose and positively impact others' lives by performing acts of kindness and service. This chapter examines the transforming potential of generosity and provides helpful advice on how to include deeds of kindness into teens' everyday lives. Teens can develop a heart of giving that improves their lives and creates a stronger sense of connection with others by helping individuals in need, working in their community, or just making a donation to a worthy organization.

In addition, giving and being grateful are powerful forces that improve bonds between people and create a feeling of community and connection. Teenagers who show others gratitude and appreciation build stronger relationships based on mutual respect and trust, which promotes a happy and encouraging social atmosphere. In a similar vein, deeds of kindness and generosity have far-reaching effects that inspire others to do the same and foster a compassionate and giving culture within communities.

Gratitude and charity have broader societal

ramifications in addition to improving one's own well-being and interpersonal relationships. Teenagers can help create a society that is more sympathetic and kind, where people help and encourage one another when they are in need, by fostering these qualities. In this chapter, we examine how giving and thankfulness can spur constructive social change and encourage young people to act as change agents inside and outside of their communities.

In the end, teens who are given the tools to practice generosity and thankfulness on a daily basis will be better able to maintain their emotional health, build stronger bonds with others, and make a positive impact on a world that is more sympathetic and caring. Teenagers can develop a giving heart that enhances their life and makes people around them happy and fulfilled by adhering to the principles of generosity and compassion, practicing appreciation rituals, performing acts of kindness and service, and modeling these virtues.

About Author

Gbogo.S. Adegboye is a versatile professional that works as an entrepreneur, manager, business economist, and motivating speaker in all of Africa.

Adegboye holds bachelor's degrees from Salfold University in Manchester, IPMA, Yale University, and Adonai University in addition to an MBA from Salfold University. Despite being born in South Africa, he presently resides in Nigeria and works as a motivational speaker for numerous organizations, businesses, and seminars. He specializes in speaking to young and aspiring managers across Africa.

Acknowledgement

First of all, I thank God alone for the successful completion of this medical composition. It would not have been possible to complete this medical book without the wisdom of God, who has been a continual source of support and guidance. I also want to thank all of my family, friends, well-wishers, and countless others that I cannot include here because they have continuously helped me in one way or another from the beginning to the end of this text.

THANKS FOR READING